Unleashing Antique Annie

A Memoir

Betty Buchanan Murphy

with Buck Buchanan

ISBN: 9798709378360

DEDICATION

Several years ago, I was a tourist in my own hometown, Chattanooga, Tennessee. A friend and I stayed at the famed "Choo Choo" and took in the local sights, including a "Duck" ride on the Tennessee River. As the skipper passed under the rocky bluffs near the old bridge, he mentioned the Hunter Art Gallery and continued his down river narrative. "Wait a minute!" I exclaimed. What about the Houston Museum?"

Where was the ghost of Antique Annie when you needed her? The making of her museum dominated the lives of our family for years. I still had the chipped treasures I bought for a bargain on its back porch. More than that, I had the memories of the tireless efforts that made an old lady's legacy a reality.

Mama and Daddy
(Irene and Blaine Buchanan)
and All the Others,
this story is for you.

Betty Buchanan Murphy
2021

ACKNOWLEDGMENTS

Thanks to my brother for his contribution to the story

Much Appreciation to Elizabeth Raber for proofreading

CHAPTER 1

Every town has its characters. Chattanooga in the late 1940's was no exception. It was the era when little girls wore white gloves to have lunch at the department store tearoom with their mothers. Often, on such trips, I'd gaze out the car window at some of the fringe personalities who frequented the downtown area of our pleasant little city in the Tennessee Valley.

There was the man, lathered with sweat, who ran up and down Market Street blowing his imaginary whistle because he thought he was a train. Another gentleman flashed the V for victory sign at every passerby. "Pore thing," my mother would say, "he doesn't know the war's over." Mama placed all the unusual types in the "Pore thing" category. Occasionally we'd see the breeze blowing the long, dark dress of a woman with washboard wave hair. Wandering the streets, she always carried a cheap suitcase and never failed to elicit a gasp when sighted by the driver of our little Ford. "Oh, there's Marla, pore thing..." Looking back, I suppose this lady was a streetwalker, but, as seven-year-olds know little of such types, I basked in the drama of seeing the local celebrity.

Occasionally characters even presented themselves at our door. One of these was Baby George, a scruffy old coot who drank from a baby bottle and begged fruit for his dirty burlap bag. Mama would hand him an apple through a crack in the door. When he turned to leave, she'd exclaim, regretting her charity, "Look at that; he's got a dozen big oranges in his sack!"

At other times, our family would seek out folks

best described as "not quite right." Since my dad was a lawyer, he was occasionally a court appointed guardian of the harmless mentally impaired, who lived in tiny outlying communities. Sunday afternoons might feature a ride in the country so he could check on his charges. We'd pull up on the gravel in front of a little gray shack. Before Daddy could open the car door, and my easily terrified mother could give the order to "roll up the window," a lanky figure would appear on the rotting porch. Daddy would shake hands, slap old "Fred" on the back, and ask about his well-being and his disability check. We usually returned home by a different route that might include visiting anything from an abandoned coal mine to an ice cream stand. I always hoped we'd end up at the consummate local attraction, Lake Winnepesaukah, a mom and pop amusement park that's still around today.

One Sunday afternoon drive to an East Brainerd suburb, however, would eclipse all the others we ever made. Even Mama climbed out of the car and squeezed through the fence this time. We heard a dog bark and saw an old lady come to the door of a ramshackle dwelling of sorts. From that time forth her concerns became a part of our family life. Her name was "Antique Annie," easily Chattanooga's most fascinating character.

Although I enjoyed the Sunday rides, I also loved to read. On this particular day I had my nose in the latest copy of Jack and Jill magazine. One story was really hard to put down. It was the serialized version of the Baba Yaga story, which ended at some climactic point to ensure the readers would spring for another issue. Baba Yaga was a Slavic witch who lived in a house that slowly revolved on its foundation of chicken feet.

Just as I reached the "to be continued" page, Daddy turned into a dirt drive. For a fleeting moment, I thought it was the entrance to Lake Winnie, where the main attraction was a creepy Boat Chute tunnel that fed the rider onto a water slide. Instead, I saw my parents heading toward a dwelling that remarkably resembled Baba Yaga's. Only the chicken feet were missing. As I hurried to catch up, especially at the sound of a ferocious dog bark, I saw the door open. I couldn't believe my eyes. There stood Baba Yaga in the flesh!

CHAPTER 2

I had two very different grandmothers. One kept her hair short and permed, ran a business, bought herself a Cadillac, and loved to travel. The other never abandoned the bun, wore older style clothing, and was content to rock on the porch. For a moment I recognized her style in the figure that stood in the doorway of the old house. There the similarity ended. I was, most assuredly, in the presence of Baba Yaga. Her real name was Anna Safely Houston. Around town she was known as "Antique Anna" or "Crazy Anna," another in the line of Chattanooga eccentrics, and yes, another of my Daddy's unusual clients, one who would call forth every ounce of his goodness, patience, and perseverance. Our whole family was to be involved in helping Ms. Houston share a legacy that nobody wanted.

"Antique Annie," as we always called her, had many husbands and several storied careers. Eventually, her love of old things became her sole obsession. I still remember walking into the musty old building. There the walking stopped because there was simply nowhere to go. The television show *Hoarders* would have had a field day, except there would have been no place for their cameras. Inside the door on the left I remember seeing an old couch with a dump site just behind. It appeared that Annie took her meals straight out of tin cans and tossed the residue on the growing pile to the rear of her only seating area. The ambiance was completed by a slop jar, which apparently comprised the bathroom. An old wood burning stove stood across the way to provide warmth and a place to "cook." A stack of paper and kindling was located conveniently and dangerously close by.

The rest of the house was filled with massive pieces of furniture, which, in turn, held every kind of glassware, artifact, and gadget imaginable. Noting pitchers tied to the ceiling overhead, I prepared for a concussion at any moment. Smaller pieces were piled on larger ones everywhere. There were antiques and curiosities, to use a trite expression, as far as the eye could see. One's vision, however, blurred after a time in the mingled atmosphere of dog odor, wood smoke, dust, and slop jar.

After being introduced to the old lady I could only describe as peppery, I summoned the courage to ask if she had any china dolls. Instead of replying, she plunged somewhere into the depths of the building off to the right. Soon I heard the wonderful sound of an old music box filling the rooms. She never answered my question.

I chalked up the visit to the strange old house as just another Sunday afternoon outing. Daddy's weekend drives were always full of surprises. This one was different: it turned out to be the first chapter of a very long story in our family history. Although Annie wanted to donate her massive collection of treasures for the public to enjoy, they were to remain in the large, makeshift building for almost a decade after her will was signed in the 1950's.

CHAPTER 3

Even before Daddy inherited Ms. Houston as a client from a colleague, our family had a reverence for the past. The house was filled with old furniture from Mama's forebears in Middle Tennessee, and I am still sorting through the papers and pictures that belonged to my great grandfather. My books are at home in the barrister bookcases that once held legal volumes in the James Building offices of Blaine Buchanan, attorney, who bought them from a mentor retiring after 50 years of practice. By the time of our visit to the shabby building on Wentworth Street, I had been in many antique stores. My youthful ambition was to own a pump organ like the one belonging to a great aunt, a dream that was eventually realized when I lived in Texas.

Chattanooga was a historic town, full of Civil War monuments and Native American lore. As a student at Missionary Ridge Elementary, I played around monuments near the school. My first boyfriend, who lived down the way, had a cannon permanently pointed at his front door. In the valley just under the Ridge a military school discovered many Civil War artifacts while excavating for a new building.

Other hills and mountains surrounding the town sported similar reminders of the historic past. In spite of this valuable heritage, city fathers and state governments preferred focusing on progress rather than preservation. I remember when a beautiful old church was torn down and replaced with a parking lot in the name of urban renewal.

Another was eliminated, all but the bell tower, which still stands as an incongruous sentinel on the corner of a main street.

Cameron Hill was one of the landmarks that figured in the town's local history. Once a Cherokee lookout point, it was later the home of a prominent artist, and then a Confederate stronghold until the city fell to advancing armies. Its elevation afforded visitors a scenic view of the Tennessee River Valley below. Then came the Interstate, which was originally planned to skirt the municipality of Chattanooga. Progressive City Fathers thought they had a better idea. Why not bring it through the town to enhance the local economy? Why not indeed? The proposed route would take the new roadway over the once embattled Cameron Hill. Opposition to the new plan raged. I remember watching the issue debated on local television because Daddy spoke on behalf of preserving the historic site. Those, like him, who wanted to fend off the opportunistic road builders were outvoted by the economic establishment who allowed steamrollers over the historic hill. In recent years "progress" has prevailed further. A large Blue Cross headquarters now perches on the remaining heights where the Cherokee warriors once surveyed the valley below. After seeing the new corporate building, I vowed to bleed to death rather than avail myself of that brand of health insurance.

The Chattanooga "powers that be" were equally stubborn about cultural matters when it came to   an opportunity for preserving the past in the form of creating a museum of "Crazy" Annie's collection. Although Daddy was good at twisting arms, he was unable to overcome their distaste at being associated with the eccentric old woman. Plan B would involve a long journey before visitors to the *Museum of Decorative Arts* on High Street would take the Fourth Street exit off the Interstate, just across from Cameron Hill.

CHAPTER 4

Although I didn't know it at the time, the family's visit to Annie's self-built house was my dad's initial contact with his client. Being forewarned about her eccentricities, he had armed himself with ice cream, having heard food gifts were appreciated. He was unfamiliar with Baba Yaga, but the warning issued in the crow like voice of the black clad specter waving her broom, was enough to give pause to anyone. Daddy always had a plan. He decided to use a military technique he called, "approach and be recognized." His explanation, of being there as an attorney to make her will, secured us the grand tour of the cavernous edifice, a two-story structure brimming from attic to cellar with items to be bequeathed. On the spot Ms. Houston's new lawyer ruled out itemizing the inventory of her thousands of relics in any legal document. He also learned that in addition to a dog and a broom, Annie had another security system. Since every item was covered with dust, she could immediately notice if something had been moved. Any clean space put her on instant alert.

Even though Ms. Houston had received a cold shoulder from the City Fathers, she was popular among the ladies belonging to the town's s civic and country club set. Ironically, these regular customers may have been the wives of the progressives who dismissed Annie without a thought. They had urged the old woman to protect her collection by making a will that provided for an eventual museum. In time the will was written, trustees were appointed to implement its provisions, and a corporation was created to manage the affairs of a future and lasting institution memorializing Annie and her treasures. The road leading to the fulfillment of these ideas was long and rocky, but Ms. Houston had the best of attorneys for such a task—one who wouldn't give up.

Although Daddy specialized in Interstate Commerce and other legal issues, he also served as a general practice attorney for many of his clients; however, he never handled divorces. When I asked him the reason, he said, "Because you never get through with them." Was he in for a surprise when he took on the task of writing Ms. Houston's will *pro bono*. He expected to set up a simple entity with five incorporators and hand the project to others. Nothing so simple would do for "Antique Annie," who wanted her charter to have 100 signers, rather than the usual 5. Over time, one of the supporters of the future museum amassed 99 signatures and asked that Daddy conclude the list, although he had earlier refused to sign. (He knew how difficult it would be for five people to agree on policy, much less 100.) Even so, he rewarded the gentleman's perseverance and reluctantly supplied the last signature. Years later our family was still involved in making Annie's dream a reality. No divorce settlement would have taken so long.

The many detractors who considered Ms. Houston a daffy old woman, were likely mistaken, at least in part. Daddy was as amazed at her canny understanding of the legal terms and ramifications of the will as he had been earlier at her knowledge of the history and origin of the items in her collection. When she was summoned to the law office to view a rough copy for approval, she wanted to sign it on the spot. She was so insistent, that Daddy rounded up some witnesses and agreed to proceed. Later, having decided to make a personnel change in the list of trustees, Annie had the will retyped with the updated changes and signed it again.

Besides handling the will, it was Daddy's task to set up the corporation that would eventually establish the museum. A meeting was planned to take place at the *Chattanooga Electric Power Board*. When Ms. Houston reported for her shining moment, her change in appearance suited the occasion. Ordinarily her unkempt hair and long black dress made her look like a story book witch. Before the day of the meeting, however, she had visited the "beauty parlor" and selected an attractive dress for the occasion. The finishing touch was an orchid corsage, a real badge of honor in that day. Daddy, who was there to make his presentation, described her as "really pretty." It was a "feel good" moment: he had accomplished what he had set out to do. He had served his client well, and the community would benefit from the display of Annie's unusual collection. After making his remarks and explanations to the newly created corporation members, he put the duplicate papers into his briefcase, wished the new endeavor well, and returned to other matters that were always piled on his expansive desk.

CHAPTER 5

With the passage of time, I had traded Jack and Jill stories for the adventures of Nancy Drew, whose father was a criminal lawyer. I lamented that mine preferred a legal practice that involved commerce and corporations to mystery. In school my class expanded the educational process by watching from across the sea as Elizabeth II became Queen of England. Closer home there was something new. I had a baby brother. In addition to a nursery, our house had undergone other changes as well. Another of Daddy's clients was a man interested in building swimming pools using vinyl liners. When I returned from a week away at church camp, our side yard was filled with a demonstrator model.

Meanwhile, Ms. Houston had died. Her deteriorating collection still sat in the same sad location. Over the next few years Daddy received an occasional report of progress toward a museum. There appeared to be very little. A group of the people involved began selling some of the antiques, even staging sales on the grounds. The elements were taking their toll on the contents of the leaky old house. Something had to be done. By the time my brother was five, Daddy was actively involved with the project again. Eventually he found a home for the museum. He also found a new helper. As usual, the adventure began after church on one of those storied Sunday afternoon drives.

My brother, Buck, remembers piling in the 1956 Ford Victoria and being told, "We're going to see a lot of neat stuff." He was probably old enough to recognize a red flag after this remark. Often our definition of "neat stuff" didn't match Daddy's. Soon the pair was headed off a paved road onto a dirt driveway. Buck still has a vivid memory of the occasion: "Dad stopped the car about halfway down the drive, and we got out of the car. As I followed him down the dirt drive, I could see we were headed for an old wooden structure that looked like a haunted house. (At my tender age of five, I probably regarded all old houses as haunted.) The grass in the yard was as tall as I was and, no doubt, hiding something scary lurking inside. With this idea in mind, I rushed up and grabbed my dad's hand." Buck's apprehension was only heightened as he and Daddy approached the house. He recalls: "I could see the covered windows as we mounted the wooden porch, every step making an eerie sound. Dad unlocked the door and pushed it open. It gave a loud creaking sound as we stepped inside. The house had a musty smell and was full of cobwebs. Apparently, no one had lived there for years."

As Buck stood processing the sight before him, stuff piled everywhere from floor to ceiling, Daddy admonished, "Watch your step; there's a lot of glass in here, and we don't want to break anything." My brother wondered to himself, "...so why bring a 5-year-old boy with you?" With a cautious eye he surveyed his surroundings again, noting little pathways that led from room to room. It was a maze, he decided, composed of furniture stacked with junk. Big and little things, even chairs, hung on the walls. Overhead, he estimated a "million" water pitchers were hanging from the ceiling. According to Buck, "It seemed like we were there for hours as my dad went from room to room, writing on a yellow pad of paper. When I asked to use the bathroom, I was told to pee off the porch since the bathroom was broken. To this day, I'm not sure the house even had a bathroom. If it did, it was surely full of antique junk. When Dad finally said it was time to leave, I was so thankful to get out of that spooky old place. I surely didn't want to be there after dark."

CHAPTER 6

As Daddy was engaged in relocating Annie's antiques, he encountered a second challenge: finding a new home for his family. In the late 1950's another segment of Interstate was planned for the Chattanooga area, and our house was in its path. This time there was no debate. The government condemned the houses and paid a pittance to their owners. Years later, when another home was gutted by fire, Daddy said there was no comparison in terms of loss. The biggest financial hit came somewhere along I-75 between the South Moore and Belvoir Avenue exits when our swimming pool became part of a four-lane.

On a brighter note, after exploring many ideas and making many searches, Daddy had managed to secure a rental for the museum, an old home on Bluff View in Downtown Chattanooga. The Hunter Art Gallery had planned to demolish the structure to build a parking lot. Instead, it was willing to let a fellow museum "park" next door. Today that area, which overlooks the Tennessee River, is known as the "Arts District," a popular location featuring restaurants, a bakery, B&B venues, and other attractions. Daddy's great nephew was married a few years ago in one of the 13 wedding venues in the area. Annie's treasures, it seemed, would be housed in a prime location. Ms. Houston was moving up in the world.

Locating a place for the Houston collection was, like the moon landing, "one small step." In addition to changing a family home to a museum, a huge undertaking in itself, a barn load of everything had to be relocated, cleaned, sorted, inventoried, and prepared for display or storage. Every hand was needed. Following his initial visit, Buck reflects: "Over the next year dad would spend a lot of time at the 'junk house,' and, oh yes, I was dragged over there more times than I can remember. Then I was put to work wrapping glassware in newspaper and putting it in boxes. Numerous times I was told, 'Now don't break anything.' I was sure my work was a violation of the child labor laws, but Dad had his own laws when it came to me."

By this time the Buchanans were established in a new home themselves. The neighborhood had all the amenities: sidewalks for bike riding, a community swimming pool, a sledding hill, and a group of friends. At the beginning of the academic year in the fall, Buck looked forward to after school fun with his new crew. "Well, so much for that idea," he recalls. "After the first day of school, my mother picked me up and headed to the 'new' museum. Little did I know at the time, but I was destined to spend many an afternoon on Bluff View." To this day he is able to describe the building in great detail.

"As I remember, this house was an interesting place. It was a two-story brick building with stucco trim. From the driveway on the right, the sidewalk led up four or five steps, heading up to a fairly small, covered porch. A big wooden door on the left side opened into a large two-story great room. Curving along the right wall from the first floor up to the second was a big wooden staircase. Just ahead of the entrance door was what looked like a closet. Instead, it was an elevator for those who didn't want to take the stairs, and it actually worked! This was quite a cool feature and a fun ride, at least for a couple of days."

Buck remembers the rest of the first floor which, "consisted of a living room and dining room on the front side of the house. The kitchen was on the left. To the right of the great room was what appeared to be a study. It led into an enclosed sitting room on the rear side of the building. The back yard was enclosed with a three-foot wrought iron fence. The upstairs consisted mainly of bedrooms, and there may have been an attic. Beneath the house was a spooky basement. At least it seemed spooky to a little kid." When he shared this description, I couldn't believe how much Buck remembered. "I was there every afternoon for a year," he reflected, in an exasperated tone.

During his after-school hours Buck was supposed to do his homework. Daddy prescribed additional academic chores as well: learning the multiplication tables or the state capitals, reading a book, and then helping Mama do chores around the museum. He entertained himself exploring the house, riding the elevator, throwing rocks off the bluff into the river, or talking to the workers who were renovating the old building. After a time, these activities began to lose their entertainment value. Buck grew "sick and tired" of going to the museum. After all, there're only so many times you can ride an elevator up and down, and only so many rocks you can throw into the river."

According to many ministers and speakers, every family has an "Uncle Bill." Ours was a painter, one of the workers paid to repurpose and refurbish the old house. He always had a tale to tell the little boy, waiting patiently for his daily ordeal to end. Often Bill spoke in the dialect of the characters involved. "I think he did more talking than he did painting," Buck muses. "At the end of every story he would tell me he was only painting to make money and open a grocery store. If I heard that once, I heard it a million times."

At length, Buck heard his last story. Uncle Bill went to work in a grocery store, and learned to imitate the accent of its Italian owner. The museum was finally ready to receive its treasures, and the work had only begun.

CHAPTER 7

While Buck was doing time with Antique Annie and Uncle Bill, I had become a teenager, commuting across town to school by riding a couple of buses. Backpacks had yet to be invented, making it necessary to balance a huge mound of textbooks atop a heavy binder thick with homework papers. Since Bible was included in the curriculum, I had a large black copy of the Good Book in the stack. Growing up in the Bible Belt, I knew the big volume should rest atop the heap. Alas! The math and science books were smaller, and I wondered if I dared to jeopardize my soul in the interest of making the load more manageable by piling the books in order of size.

Occasionally Daddy would go out of town, and I would have the unspeakable pleasure of driving his car to school. Because Chattanooga geography is comprised of rivers and hills, almost any route includes a tunnel or a bridge. My itinerary to school made it necessary to cross the Tennessee River. Today, visitors to the Houston Museum may arrive on foot from the Northshore via the Walnut Street Bridge. In the era when cars were big as boats, we drove across its high and narrow span. The ordeal was terrifying. One of my friends, whose mode of transportation was a big Lincoln, once hit the side of the bridge. Fortunately, she didn't end up in the river, and her dad didn't discover the dent in her fender for a while.

My weekday afternoons and evenings were mainly comprised of two activities: talking on the phone and doing homework until Daddy made me go to bed. Weekends brought activities with friends and the young men who attended the area boarding schools. Many of us with established relationships had a system to save these callers the dime they used for the pay phones in the dorms. They would dial our numbers, ring once, and hang up. That would be our signal to call back. Their dime was returned to call another day. For a time, our family was on a party line with the Greek people next door. I'd pick up the phone to make a call and hear an unknown tongue. What a downer! I could be missing a "ring once" or at least a friend reporting on any newsworthy event that had transpired since the end of school at 3:00; furthermore, one needed to be conversant in Greek to be able to eavesdrop on any juicy conversations.

Another way the male boarding students were able to save money was by joining a family for Sunday lunch. In my case the free meal included a side trip to the Museum "to see how things were going." The traditional weekend drive had been replaced by a trip to Bluff View. Tomlinson's restaurant, across the street from our church, was the frequent luncheon choice. Buck and I had practically grown up eating there. I think I ordered roast beef every Sunday. When Daddy paid the bill, he had to reach around an enormous stuffed pheasant that sat on the counter. Then we were off to Antique Annie's to ride the elevator—a good place for a teen couple to exchange a bit of affection.

In the summer boarding students left. Our family took a trip that almost always included a beach. When we were at home, Daddy obviously misunderstood the term "summer vacation." He didn't like the idea of his children being idle Although there were not many jobs for teens at that time, he had just the ticket. When his secretary took days off, I was the temp, like it or not. Sometimes I worked at his office on other days as well. My cousins also were drafted as helpers. We all had in common the exasperating experience of trying to erase a typo when there were four or five copies and carbons to deal with. The *James Building*, where we honed our skills, is now on the historic register of old buildings. It was Chattanooga's first skyscraper.

I'm sure as we worked those summers, people and paperwork pertaining to the Museum crossed our paths. Having been immersed in Ms. Houston's story for a long time, I decided to try my hand at writing a song about this character of characters. The words were easy, and, somehow, I invented a tune, although I had no idea how to write music. *The Ballad of Antique Annie* was born. The lyrics reflected a bit of her history and the time in which we lived. In one stanza I sent Annie to her heavenly reward. Then I wondered if that final state had been a bit ambitious for a mortal who'd had more husbands than a person could count on one hand. Clearly, she had an obsession as well, not to mention a rather abrasive personality. I decided to add a disclaimer by the line where Annie was consigned to the afterlife.

During Annie's tenure here on earth, grocery stores and other venues offered everyone a chance to be a collector. Many housewives had small empty books designed to be filled with S&H Green Stamps. These were small stickers awarded to people who spent a certain amount of money on groceries, or later, on other items as well. The trading stamps could be swapped for merchandise in catalogue stores around the country. I still have the ceramic cannister set I acquired after amassing many books full of the tiny green awards. For some reason I decided to end my little ballad by an imaginary blending of Annie's penchant for collecting with this popular fad of the day.

Now let's sing the Ballad…..

(Just make up your own tune; that's what I did)

The Ballad of Antique Annie

Chorus: (Repeat after every verse)

Antique Annie, our poor Annie
What money she could have had,
But old Annie was bound to the past,
So, she died, neglected and sad.

In Tennessee a woman lived
As strange as you might find.
She lived as though she only had
One idea on her mind.

Old Anna Safely Houston was
Some thought her only name.
'T was antiques old, and dirt, and mold
That brought this lady fame.

Her dream was showing everyone
The beauties of the past.
Now Annie's gone to Heaven
(Would you believe Purgatory?)
And her dream came true at last.

She lived like hermits in a cave,
Her treasures all around.
Her only pleasure was antiques.
Her only friend, a hound.

Her house looked like a hurricane
Had blown it where it stood.
She lighted it with kerosene
And heated it with wood.

She always slept upon the couch
And ate a tin can feast.
Where she could see h er pitchers tied.
There were fifteen grand at least.

Old Ann was ragged when she died.
Her hair would tumble down,
But at one time her wardrobe was
The bestest in the town.

Out courtin' had old Annie gone,
Was loved by two or three.
She outlived seven husbands, and
That's more than you or me.

Poor Annie's case was oh so sad.
Her days ended in woe.
All she did was buy and sell
And watch her antiques grow.

Her thrifty ways impress us all
As we count her fans and lamps.
Just think where Ann could be today
If she had saved green stamps.

CHAPTER 8

Not long after I had tucked my attempt at tune writing inside the piano bench for storage, a better musician than I sat in front of our mahogany spinet and performed for our entertainment a hillbilly interpretation of the old hymn "Precious Memories." Dot Black, the wife of one of Daddy's clients, had recently moved to the area. She was a gifted church organist and one of the few people I knew who actually had an organ in her home. Years later I bought the little *Tom Thumb* console piano she had stored in her basement. Last summer when I left for vacation, I told the neighbors, "If the house catches on fire, rescue the piano!" Today it is an antique and a collectible in its own right. Its mellow sound makes it one of my greatest treasures.

Mrs. Black is the person I will always associate with the early days of the Houston Museum. Although there were many other hardworking volunteers and employees, her smile and enthusiasm about the amazing collection of glassware were contagious. From her I learned about art glass, bisque, and many varieties of ironstone. When I came home as a newlywed furnishing my first apartment, I'd drop by the museum and bring friends. My college roommate and I loved the store on the back porch where discards were on sale. Fortunately, our tastes were extremely different. Alice, like Mama, gravitated toward dainty china with pink rose décor. I liked earthenware crocks and Toby jugs. I think we both found the moustache and cheer cups fascinating. Many of these had messages or designations such as "Love the Giver," "For a Gift," or simply "Grandfather." Mrs. Black followed the Annie tradition of striking up a music box while we sorted treasures. She also taught us the difference between pressed glass and cut glass by flicking her finger against a vase or dish. Cut glass, we learned, rings like a bell. After acquiring this interesting bit of education, Alice became a self-appointed glass detective. Once, when she and I were wandering through a pricy antique shop, she picked up a large crystal bowl and gave it a resounding thwack. "Put that down!" I gasped, noticing that the price was $5,000.

Dot Black came by her status as one of the early museum directors by investing a lot of sweat equity in the whole enterprise. She and several other women spent countless uncomfortable hours in the drafty old building preparing the dusty treasures for transport to their new home in the "Arts District." Buck's childhood memories recount the excitement of the packing process.

"When the remodeling work was done, people began to move the old junk to the house on Bluff View. There were a million boxes to open. Most of the items were glass things like pitchers, plates, cups, glasses, serving platters, butter dishes and decorative pieces. There was a lot of old furniture as well. Then there was the "odd ball" stuff like dresses, hats, clocks, animal heads, artifacts, and a few guns, which I particularly liked; in fact, the military pieces were my favorites. I was partial to the World War I German and American helmets and loved wearing them around until Mama insisted I take the hardhats off and put them back where I'd found them. Then she'd say, 'You don't know where that's been, or who's been wearing it. You might catch lice!' My guess was that the lice had died at least thirty years before I put the helmets on my head."

Buck believes Mama and some of her Garden Club friends were the ones drawing up the plans to convert the old house into a museum. As he remembers, "Everyone was called in to assist her in opening the boxes or even to help stage the museum itself. As the setting up continued, even our house became a planning area. Our screened in back porch was a sorting place for small items. Good pieces were separated from the broken ones. Mama would try to glue some of the broken items together. The others would be sold or given away. Yes, people wanted old broken glassware."

In 1961, to Buck's relief, the Houston Museum finally opened. "I still had to go down there, but it was only a day or so a month. I knew I would never forget Antique Annie and trying to find ways to entertain myself in the midst of all of her junk."

CHAPTER 9

No matter how dull Buck's afternoons at the museum were, his rides to and from the place had, at least, some entertainment value. From my grandmother with the bun, Mama had inherited an irresistible urge to remark on the human condition. Whereas Daddy's mode of education was eradicating laziness, Mama's was oral comment and warning. Which of her children would dare try on a souvenir hat at the beach without first checking it for residue left by a helmet wearing German?

One category of "Third Street Comments" from the daily museum trips involved maintaining a reasonable body weight. "See old Fatty Arbuckle over there," Mama would admonish. "He's so fat, he can barely button his britches." On the other hand, she would call attention to the corpulent gentleman's polar opposite. "Look at that pore old woman crossing the street; she's nothing but skin and bones, bless her heart."

Sometimes the admonitions were more serious: "Look out! Old Red's over there. He's tough as nails. Lock your door!" Having escaped Red in the nick of time, Buck was directed to another character. "See that man digging a ditch. If you don't go to school, that's what you'll be doing the rest of your life." Since Mama's small passenger was headed to an afternoon of practicing the multiplication tables, he probably discounted the thought of using a pick and shovel long term.

Booster seats for the younger set were unavailable during Buck's narrated tour of Third Street; perhaps he couldn't even see out the window. When Mama said, "There goes Mr. Suttberry," however, he knew a man with his zipper down had just come into view. The legendary Mr. Suttberry always had his fly open.

In 1968 the Houston Museum had to relocate and was fortunate to acquire a house on High Street near its original location. More volunteers again stepped forward to make the transition possible. I don't remember where the collection was located when we acquired Aunt Ida. By the time of her arrival, some Chattanoogans, at least, were aware of the memorial museum and its contents. The office received an unusual call from the local railroad station. The stationmaster had an unclaimed trunk of century old dresses. Would Houston be interested?

As a history buff who had once owned "Little Women" dolls I was fascinated. Some of the ensembles were labeled. Although my memory is faulty, I seem to recall an outfit belonging to Mary Todd Lincoln and another to Jenny Lind. The acquisition would be a nice addition to Annie's collection. She would have snapped it up in a heartbeat. Even so, the display areas were as stuffed as good taste would allow. But Mama had an idea, and she needed a partner in grime. I was about to make my maiden voyage to a junkyard.

Today, when we want to know anything, we pull out a device and search. A moment ago, for example, I decided to look for a descendant of Mr. Suttberry and located someone on Facebook who seemingly had solved the zipper problem by turning to sweatpants. (I confess. I copied the picture and sent it to Buck.) Now I find myself wondering how people traced items such as castoff department store mannikins. I doubt they were listed in the yellow pages.

The last time I was in Chattanooga, the department stores had all been repurposed into different venues. Darn! I could have used a hot fudge sundae from Miller's Mezzanine. Once, however, glass windows along

Market and Broad displayed wardrobe items, except at Christmas when motorized fantasy took over. Clothing was worn by manikins with adjustable parts and strange but elegant and expressive hands, just the ticket for a Mary Todd or a Jenny.

The junk yard, not to be confused with a dump containing banana peels and rotten eggs, was in Cleveland, thirty miles up the road. It was an enormous pile of furniture parts, old buckets, and just about anything else one could imagine. I seem to remember, perhaps, car doors, but not entire vehicles. Sure enough, cast offs from the big window of Loveman's Department Store lay among the ruins. Spying body parts, Mama led the charge. We gathered all the mannikin pieces we could find in the hope of creating at least one elegant lady capable of displaying a historic creation. Back at home we attached our finds and eureka! Aunt Ida was born. For a few of her limbs, we had a pair and a spare. These, along with other choice items were still stashed in the attic when I cleaned out the Buchanan house years later.

I don't remember if our new family member was ever able to sport a fashion of yesteryear. A close examination of the historic dresses revealed tiny bodices. In Mary Todd's day, ladies wore tight fitting corsets that enabled them to fit into micro waisted attire. Although Aunt Ida was no cow, she was probably designed to set forth the free-flowing styles of the '60's, perhaps even a pair of culottes. In the same way her male counterpart would never have been able to squeeze into a suit of armor. The Knights of the Round Table might have been as tough as Old Red, but they were nowhere near as large.

While Our Lady of the Junkyard awaited her chance at display stardom, she was pressed into service as part of the home security system. Mama was always on duty to protect herself from the criminal element she sensed was lurking behind every pillar and post. In her era cars had package shelves beneath the rear window. For a trip of any distance, she made sure to deposit a man's fedora on that space in full sight of the car behind. Should some *ne'er do wells* be trailing her with the thought of stealing her purse, they were to assume the presence of a male protector in the vehicle. He had simply removed his hat and was taking a nap in the back seat. I added this tactic to my arsenal of preemptive strategies with which I had been raised. I already knew, for example, a lone woman should never enter a "picture show" (as a movie theater was called then) without first equipping herself with a large hatpin. When the inevitable offender in the next seat reached over to fondle a leg, the long weapon was at the ready to pierce his errant hand.

My brother and I grew up with the expectation of looking under every bed and in every closet for miscreants any time Daddy was on a business trip. On such occasions, Mama usually called in reinforcements: the cousins from across town. They were younger than I and slightly older than Buck, who was armed, incidentally, with a pocket-knife from the Bible Book store. It had a *Love One Another* logo on the cover. Meanwhile the cousins' presence helped cut the time needed for bed and closet inspection. For their bravery in the line of duty, Mama took us to the *Krystal* for supper. We had to wolf down our burgers rather quickly to get home before dark.

Many years later I broke a road trip by spending the night with one of our former bodyguards. It so happened that her husband was out of town as well. Just before bedtime, she went to the closet and whipped out a sturdy plank with cloth padding on each end. After she wedged it between the door and the wall, she looked at me and said, "Your mother." I understood.

While awaiting her debut in Mary Todd's White House attire, Aunt Ida became our new sentinel. Mama sat her by the window where her shadow would be visible through the curtains. The malefactors casing our house must have wondered why she never left her post. Need I mention she was wearing a man's hat? Daddy learned to travel bareheaded in all sorts of weather.

Meanwhile, the Houston Museum was on its way, with or without its vintage clothing display. Chattanoogans had become supportive. The all-important volunteers had maintained their commitment. Visitors gave rave reviews. Occasionally Mama mailed me newspaper clippings pertaining to Annie's collection. When visiting at home for the holidays, I'd hear Museum news firsthand. At Christmas dinner I knew to expect at least one serving dish that had been a back porch treasure of Annie's: a covered china bowl decorated with pink roses. I always hoped Uncle Bill would handle it carefully.

CHAPTER 10

In the summer of 2018, Alice and I spent a few days in Chattanooga. For us, a visit to the Houston Museum was a must, although it was only open Wednesday through Sunday. We had to head back to Memphis, so I could catch a plane the following morning. Our only chance for a quick tour came in the middle of such a horrendous downpour, we wondered whether the doors would be opened at all. What a pleasant surprise it was to be ushered inside, meet the current director, and learn about the progressive programs and the plans for the future. As a teacher, I was pleased to know there were activities for the younger set. Maybe Buck should drop by some afternoon after school.

I looked for the Mammy Bench cradle and saw again the plates in the set of china, each one telling part of the story of an unlucky maiden. Amid many improvements, the surroundings still seemed familiar. I wondered how many willing hands still washed the glorious glassware or donated their effort in other ways. When I spotted the cut glass, I was careful to steer Alice to a different exhibit.

According to Buck, the museum claims to have over 15,000 antique pieces of the estimated 20,000 he saw on his first visit to the old house. His five-year-old eyes only saw a lot of "junk." Now he remarks, "If you think about it, that is an amazing amount of anything for one little old lady to accumulate in one lifetime," to which I add, Baba Yaga has done herself proud.

Mama and Daddy now rest side by side in White Oak Cemetery. Uncle Bill sleeps nearby. Mrs. Black is playing for a heavenly choir. Those who pioneered the early days of the museum are still remembered for the amazing feat of enabling the sharing of Annie's treasures. The torch they passed seems to be growing ever brighter in a town that truly appreciates its arts district.

All that remains of Aunt Ida is a hand missing a finger. Mama painted it green and used it to give me a new watch one Christmas. The same year she presented me with a legitimate Toby jug with no chips. Even on the back porch bargain table it cost $25.00. Other pieces she cherished now decorate my townhouse or reside in the old china cabinet she brought back from Middle Tennessee.

The weather was still windy, rainy, and foggy as Alice and I turned toward Memphis. I was glad we weren't heading across the Walnut Street bridge. For me it was a nostalgic moment. In the mist I seemed to see ghosts of the past. Was that dark shadow a wisp of Marla's dress? I had already locked my door against the possibility that Red's hard as nails grandson was hanging around nearby.

Just as we reached the outskirts of town, the clouds parted for a moment, and there, clear as day, I saw an old man with his fly open. If Mama had been there, she would have said: "There goes Mr. Suttberry,…"

Be sure to visit the
Houston Museum of Decorative Arts
201 High Street
Chattanooga, Tennessee 37403
423-267-7176

Be careful: there's a lot of glass in there.
You don't want to break anything!

ABOUT THE AUTHORS

Buck Buchanan is the president of Buchanan Business
Consulting based in Marietta, Georgia. He is a noted
speaker and the author of two book:
First and Thirty and The Game of Sales.

Betty Buchanan Murphy is an educator living in Bucks
County, Pennsylvania, and the author of
Martha's Prayer Book.

Both are native Chattanoogans.

www.ingramcontent.com/pod-product-compliance
Lightning Source LLC
Chambersburg PA
CBHW060924130726
48001CB00006B/2398